Goodnight God

Archway Publishing books may be ordered through booksellers or by contacting:

Archway Publishing
1663 Liberty Drive
Bloomington, IN 47403
www.archwaypublishing.com
844-669-3957

ISBN: 978-1-6657-4721-9 (sc)
978-1-6657-4722-6 (e)

Library of Congress Control Number: 2023913348

Print information available on the last page.

Archway Publishing rev. date: 10/24/2023

Goodnight God

Julie Stephens

Thank you God
For:

For My Dad, who's love, friendship, guidance, laughter, talents, and warm heart has influenced me and continues to touch my family and I every single day. He is so missed by all of us.

For My Mom, who taught me how to be strong and is an enormous influence on my religious faith, work ethic, and generosity. She has been missed all these years.

For My Husband, Jim, who has given me partnership, love, and support. What a life we have been blessed with!

For My Children: Maggie, Bella, and Gavin, truly my everything. They are your greatest gift to me. My love for them in never ending and I continue to learn so much about the resiliency of love through them.

For The Rest Of My Family and Friends, You have given me so many special people to laugh and grow with. They also support me in prayer and provide comfort in times of need.

1

This Book Is A Gift:

For_____

From_____

A Note To Parents and Caregivers

This book is the perfect way to end your night with your children. You will connect with them and learn about their day. They will learn how to pray. And, as a bonus, its' repetitive phrases and words will help with sight word recognition and early literacy skills.

Use the rectangles you see

throughout the book for your children

to tape on a special drawn picture

or photograph.

How Do You Pray To God?

It is just like having a conversation with a best friend.

What do you want to tell Him about your day?

What are you grateful for?

Is there something that is making you upset or worry?

God wants to hear all about it!

This book will help you have a conversation with God!

Dear God,
Before I go to bed and
before my prayers are said,
I want to thank you
for my day.
It was special in
many ways.

Goodnight God!

Thank you for my family!

My family teaches me about love.

I learned about love today when

_____.

Goodnight

God!

Thank you for my friends.

My friends are there for me and make life fun.

Tonight, I'd like to tell you about my friend

_____.

Goodnight God!

Thank you for
SMILES and LAUGHS!

I love to smile and laugh.

Today, I smiled when _____.

Something that made me laugh was

_____.

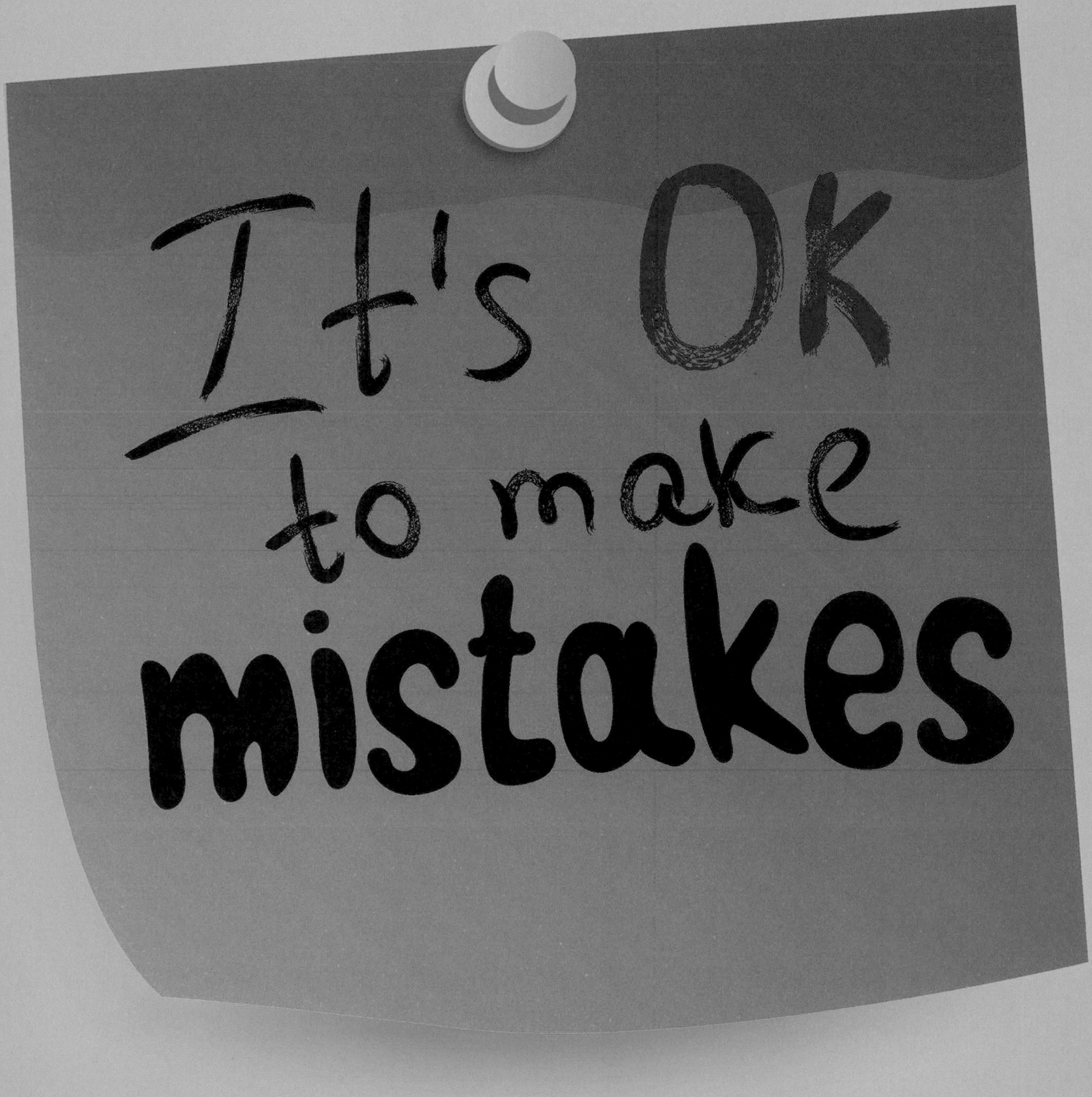
It's OK
to make
mistakes

Goodnight God!

Thank you for mistakes and tears.

Through mistakes,
I learn that nobody is perfect and that is ok.

My tears help me to let you know that I am sorry.
A mistake I'd like to talk about is

_____.

Goodnight God!

Thank you for great, big hugs.

Big hugs are a way of showing love to one another.

I really love giving hugs _____

and it makes me feel _____ .

Goodnight God!

Thank you for learning.

There are so many things
for us to learn everyday.

One thing I learned today is

_____.

Goodnight God!

Thank you for animals,
big and small, from ladybugs to bears,
for wild animals and pets!

The animal I love the most is

_____ .

Goodnight God!

Thank you for all the beautiful flowers and trees!

They are like beautiful paintings you created in nature.

My favorite flower or tree is

_____ .

Goodnight God!

Thank you for raindrops and Clouds!

Raindrops are your way of giving water to all living things.
And it reminds us to be calm and rest.

When it is raining, I really like to

_____ .

Goodnight God!

Thank you for sunny days!

The sun is so beautiful and happy!

I enjoy sunny days by

_____.

Goodnight God!

Thank you for restful nights!

It is during these restful nights
that we dream and grow!

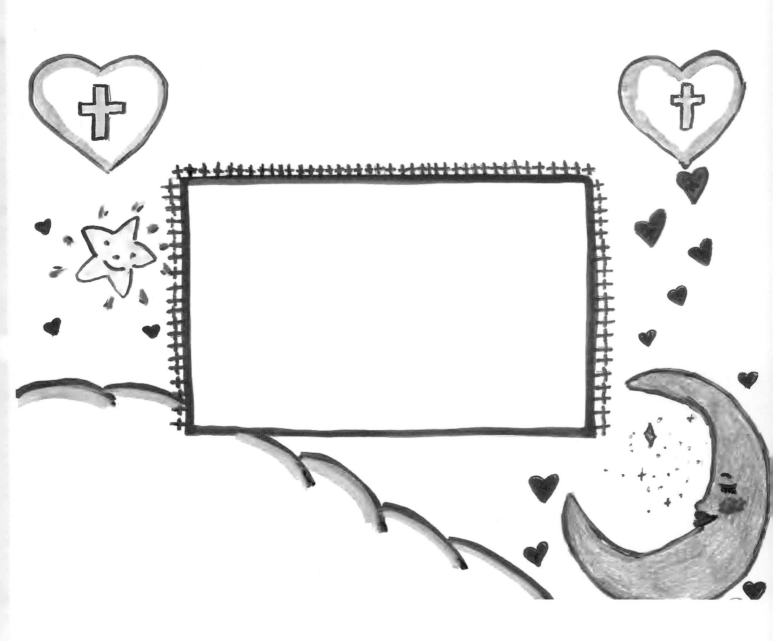

A dream I'd like to tell you about is

_____ .

Goodnight God!

Thank you for you!

You help me in so many ways.

Tonight, I'd like to say a special prayer for

_____ .

Thank you God, I love you!

Printed in the United States
by Baker & Taylor Publisher Services